Birthday Thief

Practicing the Unvoiced TH Sound

Juliette Johnson

Rosen
PHONICS
READERS

Rosen
Classroom™

I just had a birthday.

I got many things
for my birthday.

My birthday gifts are gone.
Who took my birthday gifts?

4

A thief is on the loose!

Who is the birthday thief?

I think about my birthday party.

Thirteen friends were
at my birthday.

Are there thirteen thieves?

My friends are not thieves!
I think of more clues.

I look at Thad.
Thad is my dog.

Thad has my birthday gifts.
Thad is the birthday thief!